GREATEST MOVIE MONSTERS™

DRACULA
AND OTHER VAMPIRES

T0017449

HEATHER MOORE NIVER

rosen publishing's
rosen
central®

Published in 2016 by The Rosen Publishing Group, Inc.
29 East 21st Street, New York, NY 10010

First Edition

Library of Congress Cataloging-in-Publication Data

Niver, Heather Moore.
Dracula and other vampires/Heather Moore Niver.—First edition.
    pages cm.—(Greatest movie monsters)
Includes bibliographical references and index.
ISBN 978-1-4994-3525-2 (library bound)—ISBN 978-1-4994-3526-9 (pbk.)—ISBN 978-1-4994-3527-6 (6-pack)
1. Vampire films—History and criticism—Juvenile literature. I. Title.
PN1995.9.V3N57 2015
791.43'675—dc23

2014046124

Manufactured in the United States of America

On the cover: Christopher Lee stars in "Horror of Dracula," 1958.

CONTENTS

THE VERY FIRST VAMPIRES

The word *vampire* may summon up images of a cold, dark castle, deep in the distant countryside of Hungary, and a black-caped figure who lurks in the shadows, with pale skin and a pair of bared white fangs. But this description of a vampire was popularized by one author—Bram Stoker. Before him, there were many vampire stories with a diverse cast of creatures, but all with one familiar trait: a lust for blood.

MYTHS, LEGENDS, AND LORE

Vampire stories have been around for thousands of years, though the word *vampire* became popular only in the seventeenth and eighteenth centuries. Traditionally, vampires are created by being bitten by another vampire, but other methods have been suggested, such as witchcraft and—believe it or not—a cat jumping over a corpse. Count Dracula, the vampire in Bram Stoker's novel *Dracula* (1897), popularized the vampire genre and created a vampire type with some basic similarities. Mysteriously brought back to life after death, vampires, also known as the undead, rise at night from the grave or a coffin filled with the soil of their native country. Under the cover of darkness, these gruesome (or gorgeous, depending on the story-teller) creatures feed on human blood. Stoker-type vampires also do not make a shadow or have a reflection.

Bela Lugosi (shown here with Elizabeth Allan) played the character of Dracula as a mysterious, sexy monster with his dramatic black cape and Hungarian accent.

Vampires are known for their speedy healing abilities and can fend off most human diseases. Count Dracula in Stoker's novel also traps his victims with mind control (also called glamouring in modern vampire novels) and the ability to shape-shift, such as into a bat—also a popular characteristic in vampire lore.

But vampires have weaknesses, too. Stoker gave future vampire writers plenty to choose from. He introduced the heart as a vulnerable spot—probably the most popular way of killing a vampire is to stab it through the heart with a wooden stake. Potential victims could also fight off vampires with garlic plants such as wild rose and mountain ash. Stoker's Dracula becomes calm when he touches the beads of a crucifix. The crucifix, as well as other religious items, could also take his power away. Beheading will also stop a vampire in its tracks. Another popular vampire trait is that they are killed by sunlight, but Stoker's count appears during the day on many occasions in *Dracula*. This particular trait was cemented into vampire history by films such as *Nosferatu* (1922).

LAMATSU

Most vampire legends begin in ancient Mesopotamia, four thousand years ago. The Assyrians and Babylonians cowered in fear of a nasty demon goddess named Lamatsu. Her name means "she who erases." She preyed on humans, and legends say that under the cover of darkness Lamatsu would sneak into homes to steal and kill babies, even the unborn! Researchers believe that these stories were created to explain miscarriages and infant deaths. Adults were in danger from this mythical monster, too. Stories of Lamatsu creeping in to suck the blood of young men were told in hushed whispers. The men could be left sterile, with diseases, or plagued by nightmares.

LILITH

Lilith, who is often known as the first woman on Earth, according to Jewish religious texts, is also sometimes credited with being a vampire. She wanted equal standing with Adam because they were created the same way. Some stories tell of Lilith leaving Eden and having many children. God's angels vowed to kill one hundred of her children every day until she returned. Furious, Lilith killed Adam's human children to get back at the angels. Other Lilith stories seem to take their details from the Lamatsu literature. Like

This 1864 birth amulet was created to protect newborns. It depicts an angel and has a spell against the evil eye as well as an incantation against Lilith.

Lamatsu, she has wings and sharp claws. Lilith also steals children, born and unborn, in the dead of night. Lilith appears in the television series *True Blood*, as the very first vampire.

GLOBAL VAMPIRES

Vampire legends appear all over the world. Similar stories show up in the Caribbean in the form of the soucouyant, also known as Ole Higue or Fire Rass depending on the island. By day she is a quiet old woman who often lives alone. But come nightfall she rises as a brilliant, blood-drinking ball of fire that flies through the night in search of her victims.

In China, a kue'i appeared when someone's "lower spirit," or p'o, did not pass into the afterlife, usually because they behaved badly during his or her life. The furious p'o would bring its body back to life and attack people at night. A very nasty version of the kue'i, called a Kuang-shi or Chiang-shi, was covered in white fur and had red eyes that glowed in the night.

STOKER'S INSPIRATIONS

Bram Stoker's *Dracula* came from a nightmare Stoker had about a vampire rising from its tomb. He may have also been inspired by Joseph Sheridan LeFanu's Gothic novel *Carmilla* (1872). In this novel, a woman named Laura befriends and becomes the object of romantic gestures by the female vampire Carmilla. There are also two historical figures who may have provided Stoker with ideas for his book.

Stoker had already outlined the novel when his research unearthed Vlad III Dracula (1431–1476) of Transylvania, a fifteenth-century prince. Also known as Vlad Tepes, he was

THE SCIENCE OF DRACULA

Myths about vampires were likely created to explain various mysteries. The word *vampire* first appears in Europe in the seventeeth and eighteenth centuries. The decomposition of dead bodies may have baffled early civilizations, which created vampire stories to explain the process. When the body shriveled up after death, making teeth and nails more prominent, it may have looked like growing fangs or lengthening claws. A bloated body from gasses released after death might swell organs and make blood seep out of a corpse's lips and mouth.

There were also many stories of "walking corpses" in medieval Europe during times of widespread disease, such as tuberculosis. People blamed the first person to come down with this disease. They decided he or she was a vampire and would drive a stake through his or her heart. Because lots of gases had built up in the dead body, when it was staked it would move and make a groaning sound, terrifying the living!

The disease porphyria has been attributed to some early vampire lore. In one type of this disease (there are three), patients' skin is very fragile and sensitive to light. This has led some to link the disease with early ideas of vampirism. However, the disease has many other un-vampire-like symptoms, which make this link unlikely.

known to be so cruel that he tortured and impaled his victims, even roasting children and feeding them to their mothers before impaling the women. Tepes was rumored to dine among the bodies of his victims, dipping his bread in their blood. In Stoker's novel, it's implied that Tepes was a relative of the count,

This engraving shows Vlad III Dracula enjoying dinner among his victims' impaled bodies as more people are killed. Bram Stoker was inspired by some of these terrifying tales.

but he is called Voivode, not Vlad. For all his violence, Vlad Tepes wanted to be remembered as a saint!

Stoker may have also based his story in part on a Hungarian countess named Elizabeth Báthory. During the sixteenth and seventeenth centuries, she was said to have murdered young women and bathed in their blood in hopes of staying young forever.

STOKER'S STORY

Bram Stoker's novel is widely considered the basis for most modern ideas of vampires in movies and pop culture. Stoker's

FANG FICTION: FIRST VAMPIRE PROSE AND POETRY

Characters with vampire characteristics first appear in eighteenth- and nineteenth-century poetry, such as in Heinrich August Ossenfelder's *Der Vampir* (1748) and Lord Byron's *The Giaour* (1813). The first known vampire story ever published was *The Vampyre* (1819) by John Polidori. (This story was written as a competition between Polidori, poet Percy Shelley, and Mary Shelley, who penned the famous novel *Frankenstein* during this competition.) In 1928, Ali Riga Seifi published *Kasigli Voyvode* ("The Impaling Vampire"), the only novel before 1960 that seems to have featured Count Dracula specifically. He makes appearances in short stories, however, including a two-part serial by Ralph Milne Farley called "Another Dracula" for *Weird Tales* (1930).

count is a vampire who travels from his home in Transylvania to England, where he drinks the blood of innocent people to live. The novel is told through diaries and letters written by the main characters: Jonathan Harker, who is the first character to meet the count; Harker's wife, Mina; Dr. Seward; and Lucy Westenra, who eventually becomes a vampire, too. Harker teams up with a Dr. Van Helsing to bring Dracula to his end.

Stoker perpetuated the idea of a vampire that is never seen eating or drinking, never has a shadow, isn't reflected

Jonathan Harker (played by Keanu Reeves) faces off against Dracula (Gary Oldman) in the 1992 movie Dracula, *which is closely based on Stoker's story.*

in mirrors, and must be invited into a building before he can enter. From Stoker, we also get a vampire with tremendous strength, an icy grip, long teeth (fangs), and pointed finger-nails. However, some features from this novel have been dropped from descriptions of the modern monster, such as a long white moustache, bad breath, and hairy palms.

Stoker penned more vampire prose, including a short story collection, *Dracula's Guest, and Other Weird Stories* (1914), as well as other non-vampire fiction.

CHILDREN OF THE NIGHT: EARLY VAMPIRE FILMS

B ram Stoker arranged a dramatic reading of his novel, called *Dracula, or The Undead*, in order to keep anyone from stealing his work. By staging his story, he cemented his rights to its performances. Other Dracula-like stories would have to get his permission or that of his widow to dramatize the popular count.

NOSFERATU (NOSFERATU, EINE SYMPHONIE DES GRAUENS), 1922

In 1922, the earliest known film version based on Stoker's story was produced. A German film company called Prana-Film and a director named Albin Grau loved *Dracula*. Knowing it could be an amazing film, Grau hired a codirector, Friedrich Wilhelm Murnau, and a screenwriter named Henrik Galeen.

Murnau and Galeen created a motion picture quite obviously based on *Dracula*. They changed the title to *Nosferatu*.

In his silent black-and-white film Nosferatu *(Nosferatu, eine Symphonie des Grauens), director Friedrich Wilhelm Murnau used dramatic shadows to chill and thrill rapt audiences.*

Though no one is certain where this word came from, by the time the film was being made, *nosferatu* had come to be associated with the Greek word *nosophoros*, which means plague-carrier. They also changed the setting to Bremen, Germany, in 1838, the date of an actual outbreak of the plague. Names were changed, too, such as Graf Orlock instead of Count Dracula.

It is not clear whether Prana-Film didn't know that they needed to get permission from Stoker's widow, Florence, to make a movie so similar to *Dracula*, or if they didn't

MAX SCHRECK: A REAL-LIFE VAMPIRE?

Actor Max Schreck (1879–1936) played the nightmarish Count Orlock in *Nosferatu*, but the creepiness was not just in the film. To this day, a mist of mysterious rumors swirl around the life of the tall actor whose name in German means "maximum terror." Some stories portrayed Schreck as a real vampire who made a deal with his director Murnau: Schreck would play the part if he could feast on the cast after the movie was made. He played such a convincing Orlock that people thought he must be a vampire! Of course, none of this was true, but *Shadow of a Vampire* (2000), a film supposedly about the making of *Nosferatu*, played up the myth.

In real life, Schreck was known for his talent and his enthusiasm for realistic makeup and creating costumes. He was often offered the parts of strange or very odd characters. Although he went on to work in almost thirty films in his life, he really didn't make a huge splash in the film world after *Nosferatu*. But he acted in many plays in German theater, some with his wife, Fanny Normann. Schreck tended to keep to himself and was known for his strange sense of humor.

Schreck's Count Orlock inspired Stephen King's vampire in *Salem's Lot* and an evil vampire in the video series *Subspecies*. In 1992's *Batman Returns*, Christopher Walken plays a villain named none other than Max Schreck.

Max Schreck's life ended at age fifty-six. He died of a heart attack in Germany in 1936.

Max Schreck played what some say is the creepiest film vampire. In this movie still, Count Orlock is being destroyed by sunlight.

understand the law. But when Florence Stoker found out, she took legal action, claiming copyright infringement. She won her case, and in 1925 *Nosferatu* was ordered to be destroyed. It had already been sent worldwide, so a few copies were saved.

Max Schreck plays an Orlock who looks dramatically different than almost any Dracula. He is bald with long fingernails like claws. Count Orlock's teeth practically jut out of his mouth and he has pointed ears, like a rat. Orlock wears a long coat and has a jerky, awkward walk, not unlike that of a zombie. His odd walk has inspired other monsters on the silver screen, from Frankenstein to the infamous killer Michael in *Halloween* (1978).

F. W. Murnau is sometimes called the greatest German film director of all time, and critics praise his work on this movie. Critics also loved his chilling use of shadow. Most critics now view this film as a masterpiece, but at the time the reviews were split. Felicia Feaster, writing for Turner Classic Movies, notes that when *Nosferatu* was released, "*Variety* praised the film's 'extremely effective symbolism' while *The New York Times* dismissed *Nosferatu* out of hand as a 'would-be spine-chiller.'" Regardless of the reviews, audiences were thrilled by this thriller! And they still are.

DRACULA (1931)

In 1930, Universal Studios officially bought the film rights to *Dracula* from Florence Stoker. They hired Tod Browning to direct it, and it was a perfect film for a director who loved stories about outsiders. Then there was the matter of who would play the great count. The actor Bela Lugosi, who had escaped from Hungary and hardly spoke a word of English had helped Universal convince Stoker's widow to sell them the rights at a lower price. He was expected to get the part, but he was not the first choice for Universal Pictures. In fact, even though Lugosi had played the part many times before in plays produced by Horace Liveright all over the United States, he had to fight for the role! Helen Chandler was cast as Mina with less drama.

Stoker's Count Dracula was described as wearing black from head to toe, but it was Bela Lugosi's formal wear in the 1931 film that cemented what we now consider the classic vampire fashion: a tuxedo paired with a dramatic, flowing opera cape.

Although Lugosi loved playing the part, he later commented that it was both a blessing and a curse. For the rest of his life, Lugosi played very similar characters. Lugosi's son and mother had Lugosi buried in one of his capes. Although he never expressed that desire, they felt he would have appreciated it. His son owns the single remaining official Lugosi cape.

The eye-catching promotional posters quickly popularized this film, even with children. It showed Lugosi as a monstrous, clawing predator and female characters as unsuspecting victims.

Dracula was so popular that it resulted in several sequels: *Dracula's Daughter* (1936), starring Gloria Holden, and *Son of Dracula* (1943), starring Lon Chaney Jr. John Carradine played the count in both *House of Frankenstein* (1944, also starring Boris Karloff and Lon Chaney Jr.) and *House of Dracula* (1945, with Onslow Stevens).

UNDER THE SPELL OF *DRÁCULA*: THE SPANISH FILM

At the same time the American *Dracula* was being filmed, a Spanish-language version, *Drácula*, was being made. In an interview, Lupita Tovar Kohner, who played the character of Eva (Mina in the American film), explains that the American cast and crew worked all day, then the Spanish cast would come in and work all night. At night on the dark set they were "under the spell of Dracula," she explains in the "Introduction to the Spanish Version of *Dracula*" of the *Dracula* Legacy Series DVD. The two crews and casts used the same sets and even the same marks on the floors to indicate where the actors should stand. However, the wardrobes were different for the two films. Kohner noted that the American Mina wore very modest outfits, whereas her own costumes for Eva were far more revealing.

The Spanish version may have had an advantage over the American film. They were able to watch what the Americans filmed each day. This gave them the opportunity to improve on it. Many critics like the lively performance that Carlos

HAMMER HORROR

In 1958, Hammer Films created a gruesome and realistic portrayal of the count in *The Horror of Dracula*, starring Christopher Lee. This film was very graphic and not shy about the sexuality of vampires. *The Horror of Dracula* was such a hit that Hammer went on to offer *The Brides of Dracula* (1960), *Dracula, Prince of Darkness* (1966, again starring Lee), and *Dracula Has Risen From the Grave* (1968), among others, each generally saucier than the last.

Villarías gave as the count (Conde Drácula) under the direction of directors George Melford and Enrique Tovar Ávalos. Some of the visual effects and smooth camera work make critics and film fans prefer the look of the Spanish version. The camera has a more fluid movement, making the dark moods of the story more dynamic. *Drácula* turned out to be one of the last Spanish-language films made in Hollywood.

NEW *NOSFERATU*

In 1979, Count Orlock returned in *Nosferatu: The Vampyre* (Originally titled *Nosferatu: Phantom der Nacht*). This *Nosferatu* remake was written, produced, and directed by Werner Herzog and featured Klaus Kinski as the creepy Count Orlock. It kept the same basic storyline as the 1922 film, but it restored the names to those used in Stoker's novel, this time with permission. In 1988 an Italian sequel was made, called *Vampire in Venice*.

*Christopher Lee starred as the count in **The Horror of Dracula** (1958) for Hammer Films. Hammer produced graphic seductive vampire films that delighted the audiences.*

E. Elias Merhige created the film *Shadow of the Vampire* (2000) out of respect to Murnau and *Nosferatu*. This film is a comedy that takes a look at the making of the movie. Willem Dafoe played Max Schreck and won an Oscar for Best Supporting Actor for his performance.

MORE CHILDREN OF THE NIGHT: MODERN VAMPIRES

On September 27, 1949, Bela Lugosi performed as a guest star on *The Texaco Star Theater*, becoming the first person to appear on television dressed as a vampire, although he was not specifically called Dracula on the program. Vampires didn't become part of regular television entertainment until the early 1950s, however, because television was supposed to amuse, not frighten, viewers.

VAMPIRES FOR THE VERY YOUNG

Most vampire movies and stories are created for an adult audience, but as the first popular fang film, *Dracula*, showed, kids have always loved the story! It wasn't until 1971 that the first novel with a vampire theme was written just for a young audience. *Danger on Vampire Trail* (Hardy Boys, #50, 1971) was part of the mystery series by Franklin W. Dixon. Angela

They're Not Just Best Friends.
They're Blood Brothers.

The Little Vampire

In 2000 The Little Vampire film finally brought the popular kids' book series, originally published in 1979, to the silver screen. It was also a television series in 1986.

Sommer-Bodenburg's twenty-book series *The Little Vampire*, the first of which was published in 1979, inspired a movie of the same name that was released in 2000.

On the cuddlier side, children's authors Deborah and Frank Howe created *Bunnicula* (1979) about a fanged vampire bunny that sleeps all day and sucks the juice out of vegetables. Frank continued the book as a series, which ended with *Bunnicula Meets Edgar Allen Crow* in 2006. He also did picture book spin-offs for even younger readers, *Tales from the House of Bunnicula* and *Bunnicula*

COUNTING WITH COUNT VON COUNT

Sesame Street's Count von Count lives in a castle, has bats for pets, wears a cape that Bela Lugosi would love, and has fangs.

It's true, the purple puppet does not have many of the vampire's nastier habits, like drinking blood, but he has an obvious attraction to counting. *Sesame Street* didn't invent this fascination with numbers just to teach kids to count. A common vampire weakness in legends is a compulsive need to count things, also known as arithmomania. In pre-modern days when most people feared that vampires were a real threat, they would sprinkle rice or poppy seeds all over the floor. When the vampire entered their homes, they thought it would be unable to resist counting every last seed or grain. This distraction would leave enough time for the humans to escape or the sun to rise.

and Friends. A television cartoon, *Bunnicula, the Vampire Rabbit*, aired in 1982.

Other cartoon vampires include a small purple vampire named Little Gruesome in Hanna-Barbera Productions' *Wacky Races* (1968–1970), *Archie's Weird Mysteries: Archie and the Riverdale Vampires* (2001), and *Scooby-Doo and the Legend of the Vampire* (2003), just to name a few.

Sesame Street's cast of muppets includes Count von Count (although he's never actually called a vampire), who counts everything he can, whether it's his pet bats or bananas. And kids' breakfast cereals even get in on the vampire trend with Count Chocula.

VAMPIRES IN THE LIVING ROOM

In the 1960s, television started to include vampires as characters in leading roles. *The Addams Family* (1964–1966) on ABC was based on the Charles Addams cartoon featured in the *New Yorker* magazine. The curvy and feisty Morticia Addams was played by Carolyn Jones and later by Ellie Harvey in *The New Addams Family* (1998–1999). Morticia was not specifically called a vampire, but her gothic appearance, with pale skin and long, black dresses, made the suggestion.

Another successful series was *The Munsters* (1964–1966) on CBS, which centered on a wacky family that included a vampire duo. Yvonne de Carlo played Lily Munster and Al Lewis was Grandpa Munster. As the series progressed, viewers found out that Grandpa was supposed to be Count Dracula!

DARK SHADOWS

In 1966, television viewers were introduced to the Collins family in *Dark Shadows* (starring Jonathan Frid and Grayson Hall). At first, it was just a gothic daytime drama, but when ratings were poor, they added some ghosts. However, it was the addition of the vampire that really made the show a success. Teens rushed home from school to see the next episode. Jonathan Frid played the unhappy vampire named Barnabas Collins. The show boasts 1,200 episodes, and it ran until 1972. In 1991 a *Dark Shadows* miniseries aired, featuring Ben Cross and Joanna Going. *Dark Shadows* also made it to the silver screen, with *House of Dark Shadows* in 1970, starring Jonathan Frid and Grayson Hall, and a remake of the original television series in 2012, starring Johnny Depp and Michelle Pfeiffer. Cross, Depp, and Frid all sport a long black Lugosi-style cape in their Barnabas Collins characterizations. Depp in particular wears a long black cape and even a medallion, as did Lugosi in 1931, and has long nails not unlike Orlock in *Nosferatu*.

BUFFY THE VAMPIRE SLAYER

In 1992 director Fran Rubel Kuzui and writer Joss Whedon brought a new vampire story to the silver screen: *Buffy the Vampire Slayer*, starring Kristy Swanson and Donald Sutherland. Buffy is a teenage girl who learns she is the chosen one of all vampire slayers. The film's reviews were mixed, but moviegoers loved it. Five years later, *Buffy* came to television, this time with Whedon as director and starring Sara Michelle Geller as Buffy Summers and David Boreanaz as her love interest Angel, who is inconveniently a vampire with a soul. Buffy slayed vampires and all kinds

Sara Michelle Geller played the butt-kicking vampire slayer Buffy Summers in the Buffy the Vampire Slayer *television series.*

of monsters for seven seasons. In an episode in 2000 titled "Buffy v. Dracula," Buffy faces off with none other than Count Dracula himself! The show also featured a super-vampire called the Master, with pale skin that hinted back to *Nosferatu*.

A darker spin-off, *Angel*, again starring Boreanaz, hit the airwaves in 1999. Other characters from the Buffy show appeared, and occasional appearances were made by Geller.

In 2007, Dark Horse Comics published the series *Buffy the Vampire Slayer* Season Eight, which continued where the television show left off. Angel was also popular enough to result in several books and comics, including the comic book series *Angel, After the Fall* by Brian Lynch in 2008, which also picks up where the television show left off.

True Blood's stars were the tough and telepathic southern belle Sookie Stackhouse (Anna Paquin) and vampire Bill Compton (Stephen Moyer). The HBO drama emphasized the violence and sex of vampire lore.

TRUE BLOOD

HBO's *True Blood* came about in part thanks to the comparatively tame *Buffy*. With its darker, sexier, and more violent themes, it appealed to an older audience but was likely just as popular as *Buffy*. Based loosely on *The Southern Vampire Mysteries* series of novels by Charlaine Harris, this series ran from 2008 to 2014. The main character, Sookie Stackhouse (played by Anna Paquin), is a telepathic waitress in Bon Temps, Louisiana. When she meets Bill Compton (played by Stephen Moyer), a 173-year-old vampire, she discovers the one man who can resist her telepathic talents.

Although the vampires in this series stay pretty traditional—they can't go out in the light and can glamour humans (a vampire trick to hypnotize victims)—Harris added a synthetic blood called "tru blood," which allows vampires to live with humans without fear of needing to drink their blood. In the fifth and sixth seasons, the series adds Lilith, who is said to be the original vampire. She tells Bill, "God made me as vampire, and Adam and Eve as human. I am worshiped as a god as some may come to worship you as a god. But there is no god but God." (Lilith has also made appearances in other vampire literature, such as the Marvel Comic *Morbius the Living Vampire*).

THE VAMPIRE DIARIES

A series called *The Vampire Diaries* (2009–), based on the book series by L. J. Smith, is geared toward a younger audience without as much violence and sexual content. Its series premier was viewed by 4.8 million in the United States. *The Vampire Diaries* has won numerous awards, as well as a nomination for the 2015 People's Choice Award for Favorite Network Sci-Fi/Fantasy TV Show.

FANG FILM

By now, the library of vampire- and Dracula-related movies is almost more than anyone could manage to watch, even if you had every night for the rest of time to do it! So let's just take a look at a few.

THE LOST BOYS

The 1980s brought the vampire film into a slightly edgier, practically punk genre with *The Lost Boys* (1987), with its tag line "Being wild is in their blood." In this horror comedy, a single mother, Lucy (perhaps a nod to the character in Stoker's

THE LOST BOYS

Kiefer Sutherland played a vampire bad boy in the 1987 **The Lost Boys.** *The vampires in this fun and funky flick were a change from formal Dracula dramas.*

story), moves to a new town in California with her two sons, played by Jason Patric and Corey Haim. Soon the boys realize that there is more to the motorcycle gangs in their new neighborhood than meets the eye.

Like Stoker's vampires, *The Lost Boys* vampires come out only at night (in fact, the actors are rumored to have done the same while they were filming, even covering their windows so they could sleep during the day). It sneered at the glamour and capes of Bela Lugosi and took on punk hair and clothes. In his article for the Total Film website, Josh Winning calls it "a vampire flick made back when vampire flicks weren't known for being edgy and fun." In this film, the vampires look like normal human beings…until they're on the hunt, when their faces become monstrous with white or blood-red eyes and sharp, grotesque features. It is an idea that Joss Whedon later used in his *Buffy* series with the character Angel.

The Lost Boys was also written as a novella in 1987 by author Craig Shaw Gardner. It includes scenes that were dropped from the film as well as some new vampire lore, such as vampires being unable to cross running water. *The Lost Boys* film won the Saturn Award for Best Horror Film in 1988.

INTERVIEW WITH THE VAMPIRE

Anne Rice's popular *Vampire Chronicles* novels began with *Interview with the Vampire* in 1976, which is credited with reviving vampire stories for a modern audience. Without her work, many believe there would be no *Buffy, True Blood,* or *Twilight.* This first novel was made into a film of the same name in 1994, starring Brad Pitt and Tom Cruise. The third book in the series, *Queen of the Damned*, published in 1988, was made into a movie of the same name in 2002, starring pop star Aaliyah in the title role. The film was released six months after Aaliyah's untimely death. In 2014, Rice released the eleventh book in the series, *Prince Lestat.* That same year, Universal Studios bought the rights to all of the books in the *Vampire Chronicles* series with the intention of making more movies.

TWILIGHT

One of the more recent films to get people talking about vampires is *The Twilight Saga* series (2008–2012), five films based on Stephenie Meyer's four-book series: *Twilight, New Moon, Eclipse,* and *Breaking Dawn.* (*Breaking Dawn* was released in two parts.) The *Twilight* books and movie focus on a budding love between a high school student Isabella (Bella) Swan (played by Kristin Stewart) and the 108-year-old vampire Edward Cullen (played by Robert Pattinson). *Twilight* vampires are described as having extreme beauty, and once a human is turned into a vampire he or she becomes even more attractive—practically perfect.

The vampires in this series do stay true to a few Stoker qualities, such as showing fangs when they turn into vampires and surviving only on blood. However, Meyer's vampires are able to go out in the daylight. But because they sparkle in the sun, staying out of direct light allows them to keep their secret safe. The vampires in the Cullen family also feed on animals rather than humans and are immune to crucifixes and holy water.

DRACULA UNTOLD

Dracula Untold (2014) goes back to the turn of the century and Vlad the Impaler's history. The movie's website describes it as "the origin story of the man who became Dracula," and the critics generally agreed. *Dracula Untold* was an action film rather than horror. This PG-13 movie only suggested some of the violence that made the historical Vlad (played by Luke Evans) quite famous in history. And although some parts of the story agree with history, *Time* magazine's entertainment writer Richard Corliss comments that it depicts "Vlad as a loving husband, a protective father and a national hero."

TRULY UNDEAD MONSTERS

Vampire stories have remained very popular through several generations. With more than two hundred interpretations of the count in film alone, Dracula is the most popular horror film character of all time. Modern styles have also taken up vampire stories, with undead creatures gracing the pages of comic books, appearing in musicals, and even being choreographed into a ballet. The vampire genre, it seems, won't die anytime soon. The only question is, where will vampires show up next?

BEAUTY AND THE BEAST

Today's Dracula characters are far more physically appealing than Max Schreck's *Nosferatu* and even Bram Stoker's hairy-palmed creature with halitosis. Stoker's Dracula becomes younger as he drinks blood, but not better looking. More recent vampires tend to be handsome, sympathetic characters, such as Bill Compton and Eric Northman in *True Blood* and Edward Cullen and the vampires of *Twilight*.

In King's novel and the 1979 film Salem's Lot, vampires looked like authentic, scary monsters.

Not all of today's modern bloodsuckers are pretty boys, however. Horror author extraordinaire Stephen King's book *Salem's Lot* harkens back to the more "authentic" book-based Dracula. He remembers:

One of the novels I taught was Dracula. I was surprised at how vital it had remained over the years; the kids liked it, and I liked it, too. One night over supper I wondered aloud what would happen if Dracula came back in the twentieth century, to America. "He'd probably be run over by a Yellow Cab on Park Avenue and killed," my wife said…. But if he were to show up in a sleepy little country town, what then? I decided I wanted to find out, so I wrote 'Salem's Lot, which was originally titled Second Coming.

The vampires of Guillermo del Toro's trilogy *The Strain* (2009–2011), as well as the television series based on the

NEW ORLEANS: VAMPIRE CITY

New Orleans has a rich history with vampire stories. It has hosted its own Vampire Film Festival, which included films, discussions with authors, and even a ball! New Orleans is the "true American vampire city," according to J. Gordon Melton, author of *The Vampire Book: The Encyclopedia of the Undead*, and with good reason. Both Anne Rice and Charlaine Harris set their stories in this city. The movies based on Rice's novels and Harris's television series *True Blood* were filmed in and around New Orleans.

books, are some gross ghouls. Molly Osberg, editor and writer for the Verge website, writes that "vampires don't look like pop stars and sip blood from champagne flutes; they rip your throat out…" And not much is pretty about that!

CREATURES IN THE COMICS

The comic book world has loved Dracula and vampire stories, too. The first vampire to bare his pointy teeth in comics was the Vampire Master. He appeared in a four-part DC Comics series from 1935 to 1936, starting with *More Fun Comics No. 6: The Vampire Master Part 1*. The first time Dracula himself appeared in a comic was in 1951 in *Eerie No. 8*.

But vampires were banned from comic books in 1954 by the Comic Magazine Association of America, and they weren't allowed out of the coffin again until 1972. The ban was all thanks to

Wesley Snipes starred in Marvel Comics' Blade trilogy. African American Blade was uniquely half-vampire and half-human, so he was not limited to going out only at night.

the idea that they were too violent and sexy and thus a bad influence on young minds. A similar ban was applied in the United Kingdom.

Marvel Comics created *Morbius, the Living Vampire* in 1971 and released it after the ban was lifted. *Fray: Future Slayer* (by Joss Whedon, of *Buffy the Vampire Slayer* fame) and *Buffy the Vampire Slayer* both tackled vampires among the comic strips, too. There's even a vampire cow out there in comic land in *Hellcow*.

And speaking of vampire slayers, there's Blade. He's an African American, as well as half vampire and half human. So he can walk about during the day. Blade first appears in the Marvel Comic *The Tomb of Dracula #10* (1973). He goes on to star in his own series of comic books and then a trilogy of movies: *Blade* (1998), *Blade II* (2002), and *Blade: Trinity* (2004) with Wesley Snipes in the title role. This was followed by a short-lived series, *Blade: The Series* (2006), starring Sticky Fingaz. *The Vampire Book* author J. Gordon Melton describes Blade as "evil, but with some traits of human feeling, pining over love betrayed...."

DRACULA STAGED

Dracula's fierce fangs have even been interpreted into dance all over the world. Canada's Royal Winnipeg Ballet performed a full-length ballet created by choreographer Mark Godden. Later, it was adapted for film as *Dracula: Pages from a Virgin's Diary*. *Dracula, the Musical*, based on the Stoker's novel, is also widely performed.

Count Dracula, whether he's depicted in the movies or elsewhere, continues to fascinate and frighten. But before you decide whether or not you truly believe in vampires, consider these parting words from Van Helsing, spoken at the end of the 1931 film: "Just a moment, ladies and gentlemen! Just a word before you go. We hope the memories of Dracula and Renfield won't give you bad dreams, so just a word of reassurance. When you get home tonight and the lights have been turned down and you are afraid to look behind the curtains and you dread to see a face appear at the window—why, just pull yourself together and remember that after all there are such things."

FILMOGRAPHY

Nosferatu (Nosferatu, eine Symphonie des Grauens) (1922)
Directed by F. W. Murnau. Starring Max Schreck and Greta Schröder.

Dracula (1931)
Directed by Tod Browning. Starring Bela Lugosi and Helen Chandler.

Dracula's Daughter (1936)
Directed by Lambert Hillyer. Starring Otto Kruger and Gloria Holden.

Son of Dracula (1943)
Directed by Robert Siodmak. Starring Lon Chaney Jr. and Robert Paige.

House of Frankenstein (1944)
Directed by Erle C. Kenton. Starring Boris Karloff and Lon Chaney Jr.

House of Dracula (1945)
Directed by Erle C. Kenton. Starring Onslow Stevens and John Carradine.

The Horror of Dracula (1958)
Directed by Terence Fisher. Starring Peter Cushing and Christopher Lee.

House of Dark Shadows (1970)
Directed by Dan Curtis. Starring Jonathan Frid and Grayson Hall.

Blacula (1972)
Directed by William Crain. Starring William Marshall and Vonetta McGee.

Dracula A.D. 1972 (1972)
Directed by Alan Gibson. Starring Christopher Lee and Peter Cushing.

Nosferatu the Vampyre (1979)
Directed by Werner Herzog. Starring Klaus Kinski and Isabelle Adjani.

The Lost Boys (1987)
Directed by Joel Schumacher. Starring Jason Patric and Corey Haim.

Bram Stoker's Dracula (1992)
Directed by Francis Ford Coppola. Starring Gary Oldman and Winona Ryder.

Buffy the Vampire Slayer (1992)
Directed by Fran Rubel Kuzui. Starring Kristy Swanson and Donald Sutherland.

Interview with the Vampire: The Vampire Chronicles (1994)
Directed by Neil Jordan. Starring Brad Pitt and Tom Cruise.

Blade (1998)
Directed by Stephen Norrington. Starring Wesley Snipes and Stephen Dorff.

The Little Vampire (2000)
Directed by Uli Edel. Starring Jonathan Lipnicki and Rollo Weeks.

Shadow of the Vampire (2000)
Directed by E. Elias Merhige. Starring John Malkovich and Willem Dafoe.

Dracula: Pages from a Virgin's Diary (2002)
Directed by Guy Maddin. Starring Wei-Qiang Zhang and Tara Birtwhistle.

Blade II (2002)
Directed by Guillermo del Toro. Starring Wesley Snipes and Kris Kristofferson.

Blade: Trinity (2004)
Directed by David S. Goyer. Starring Wesley Snipes and Kris Kristofferson.

Twilight (2008)
Directed by Catherine Hardwicke. Starring Kristen Stewart and Robert Pattinson.

New Moon (2009)
Directed by Chris Weitz. Starring Kristen Stewart and Robert Pattinson.

Eclipse (2010)
Directed by David Slade. Starring Kristen Stewart and Robert Pattinson.

Breaking Dawn Part 1 (2011)
Directed by Bill Condon. Starring Kristen Stewart and Robert Pattinson.

Breaking Dawn Part 2 (2012)
Directed by Bill Condon. Starring Kristen Stewart and Robert Pattinson.

Dark Shadows (2012)
Directed by Tim Burton. Starring Johnny Depp and Michelle Pfeiffer.

Dracula: The Dark Prince (2013)
Directed by Pearry Reginald Teo. Starring Luke Roberts and Jon Voight.

Dracula Untold (2014)
Directed by Gary Shore. Starring Luke Evans and Dominic Cooper.

GLOSSARY

ARITHMOMANIA An obsession with counting.

CHOREOGRAPHER One who creates and arranges dances and dance steps.

CRUCIFIX A symbol of the cross with a figure of Jesus on it.

DECOMPOSITION Rotting or breaking down.

GOTHIC Dark and gloomy; belonging to the dark ages.

GRUESOME Causing horror or disgust.

LORE Information or traditions about a subject.

MISCARRIAGE A medical condition in which a pregnancy ends too early for the baby to survive.

MOUNTAIN ASH A small tree in the rose family.

PORPHYRIA A rare blood disease in which a person's ability to produce red blood cells is limited.

PREINDUSTRIAL Having to do with a time before industry was built up.

PREMATURE Occurring too soon.

SPIN-OFF Something inspired by or marketed because of its relationship to a popular movie, book, or television show.

STERILITY The characteristic of being unable to reproduce.

SYMPATHETIC Friendly or enjoyable.

SYNTHETIC Made from chemicals.

TELEPATHIC Able to read minds.

TRILOGY A collection of three, usually novels, films, or plays.

TUBERCULOSIS A spreadable disease of the lungs.

FOR MORE INFORMATION

American Film Institute

2021 N Western Avenue

Los Angeles, CA 90027

(323) 856-7600

Website: http://www.afi.com

The American Film Institute seeks to protect the history of films like *Dracula*, to honor artists and their work, and to educate future filmmakers.

The Dracula Library

Center for Studies on New Religions

Via Confienza 19

10121 Torino

Italy

Website: http://www.cesnur.org/dracula_library.htm

The Dracula Library is the largest public library of vampire books, including books about vampires as well as books by authors of vampire-related books.

North American Victorian Studies Association

Dept. of English

Purdue University

500 Oval Drive

West Lafayette, IN 47907

Website: http://navsa.org

The North American Victorian Studies Association was founded to offer a forum for discussion about Victorian literature, such as *Dracula*.

The Transylvania Society of Dracula: Canadian Chapter

P.O. Box 23240

Churchill Square P.O.

St. John's, NF A1B 4J9

Canada

This international nonprofit organization studies Vlad (Tepes) Dracula as well as Count Dracula. The original chapter was formed in Romania.

WEBSITES

Because of the changing nature of Internet links, Rosen Publishing has developed an online list of websites related to the subject of this book. This site is updated regularly. Please use this link to access the list:

http://www.rosenlinks.com/GMM/Drac

FOR FURTHER READING

Abele, Robert. *The Twilight Saga: The Complete Film Archive: Memories, Mementos, and Other Treasures from the Creative Team Behind the Beloved Motion Pictures.* New York, NY: Little, Brown, 2012.

Beresford, Matthew. *From Demons to Dracula: The Creation of the Modern Vampire Myth.* London, England: Reaktion Books, 2009.

Bringle, Jennifer. *Vampires in Film and Television.* New York, NY: Rosen Publishing, 2011.

Burgan, Michael. *Dracula's Dark World* (Horrorscapes). New York, NY: Bearport, 2010.

Hellman, Roxanne, and Derek Hall. *Vampire Legends and Myths* (Supernatural). New York, NY: Rosen Publishing, 2011.

Indovino, Saina C. *Dracula and Beyond: Famous Vampires & Werewolves in Literature and Film* (Making of a Monster: Vampires & Werewolves). Broomall, PA: Mason Crest, 2010.

Kaplan, Arie. *Vampires: Dracula: The Life of Vlad the Impaler.* New York, NY: Rosen Central, 2011.

Klinger, Leslie S. *In the Shadow of Dracula.* San Diego, CA: IDW, 2011.

Roberts, Steven. *Vampires!* New York, NY: Rosen Publishing, 2012.

Sims, Michael, ed. *Dracula's Guest: A Connoisseur's Collection of Victorian Vampire Stories.* New York, NY: Walker and Company, 2010.

Stewart, Gail. *Vampires: Do They Exist?* (The Vampire Library). San Diego, CA: ReferencePoint, 2010.

Stoker, Bram. *The New Annotated Dracula.* Edited by Leslie Klinger. New York, NY: Norton, 2008.

Thomas, Roy. *Dracula* (Marvel Classics). New York, NY: Marvel, 2010.

Weingarten, Ethan. *Transylvania.* New York, NY: Gareth Stevens, 2014.

Woog, Adam. *Vampires in the Movies* (Vampire Library). San Diego, CA: ReferencePoint, 2010.

BIBLIOGRAPHY

Atkinson, Michael. "A Bloody Disgrace." *Guardian*, January 25, 2001. Retrieved November 8, 2014 (http://www.theguardian.com).

Clark, Josh. "Who Was the Real Count Dracula?" Retrieved November 15, 2014 (http://history.howstuffworks.com).

Corliss, Richard. "The Vampire as Messiah in Dracula Untold." *Time*, October 12, 2014. Retrieved November 12, 2014 (http://time.com).

Feaster, Felicia. "Nosferatu." TCM. Retrieved November 6, 2014 (http://www.tcm.com/this-month/article/437|0/Nosferatu.html).

Graham, Dave. "Book Lifts Lid on Star of Eerie First Dracula Film." Reuters, May 9, 2008. Retrieved November 15, 2014 (http://www.reuters.com).

History.com "Was Dracula a Real Person?" May 22, 2013. Retrieved November 15, 2014 (http://www.history.com).

Huber, Jennifer. "Science Behind Vampire Myths." Quest, October 29, 2012. Retrieved November 15, 2014 (http://science.kqed.org).

IMDb. "Nosferatu the Vampyre." Retrieved November 15, 2014 (http://www.imdb.com/title/tt0079641/?ref_=nm_knf_i2).

King, Stephen. "'Salem's Lot." Stephen King Official Website. 2014. Retrieved November 15, 2014 (http://stephenking.com).

Melton, J. Gordon, Ph.D. *The Vampire Book: The Encyclopedia of the Undead*. Third ed. Canton, MI: Visible Ink, 2014.

Osberg, Molly. "Special Vampires Unit: Guillermo del Toro's 'The Strain' is 'CSI' with the Undead." The Verge, July 12, 2014. Retrieved November 15, 2014 (http://www.theverge.com).

Universal Studios. *Dracula: The Universal Legacy Collection*. DVD. 2004.

Winning, Josh. "The Story Behind The Lost Boys." Total Film, March 11, 2010. Retrieved November 11, 2014 (http://www.totalfilm.com).

Zalben, Alex. "The 10 Best Vampires in Comics." MTV Geek News, February 24, 2011. Retrieved November 15, 2014 (http://geek-news.mtv.com/2011/02/24/the-10-best-vampires-in-comics).

INDEX

ABOUT THE AUTHOR

Heather Moore Niver is a writer and editor living in New York State. Among many other titles, such as *20 Fun Facts About Bats*, she has written a deliciously gory book called *Digging Up the Dead: Executions and Sacrifices*.

PHOTO CREDITS

Cover, p. 15 © Photos 12/Alamy; pp. 5, 12 © Moviestore collection Ltd/Alamy; p. 7 Gali Tibbon/AFP/Getty Images; p. 10 PHAS/Universal Images Group/Getty Images; p. 17 Hulton Archive/Getty Images; p. 19 Mary Evans/Ronald Grant/Everett Collection; p. 22 Silver Screen Collection/Moviepix/Getty Images; pp. 24, 38 © New Line/courtesy Everett Collection; p. 28 © 20th Century Fox Film Corp. All Rights Reserved/courtesy Everett Collection; p. 29 photo Prashant Gupta/© HBO/courtesy Everett Collection; pp. 31, 36 © Warner Bros./courtesy Everett Collection; pp. 40–41Andrey_Kuzmin/Shutterstock.com; interior pages banners and backgrounds Nik Merkulov/Shutterstock.com, Apostrophe/Shutterstock.com.

Designer: Brian Garvey; Editor: Tracey Baptiste